Little Polyglot Books

presents:

AT HOME

English & Norwegian

Published by Linguacious® 2020

To Dylan and Isabella

Copyright © 2020 Linguacious ®.

All rights reserved. This book or parts thereof may not be reproduced in any form, stored in any retrieval system, or transmitted in any form by any means - electronic, mechanical, photocopy, recording, or otherwise - without prior written permission of Linguacious®, the publisher.

Little Polyglot Books is a division of Linguacious®.

Linguacious ®, IA, USA

www.linguacious.net

contact@linguacious.net

Little Polyglot Books - At Home/Hjemme

English & Norwegian (Bokmål)

Note on Bokmål: Many dialects where Bokmål is the written standard treat feminine nouns as masculine nouns, grammatically. In this material, we employ the common approach of using the indefinite article "et" with neuter nouns and the indefinite article "en" with both masculine and feminine nouns, instead of using the indefinite article "ei" with feminine nouns.

The Linguacious name and logo are a federally registered trademark of Linguacious®.

Little Polyglot is a trademark of Linguacious®.

 www.facebook.com/linguacious

 www.twitter.com/linguacious_llc

 www.instagram.com/linguacious_llc

Playing the Audio

Two different ways to hear the audio for each word:

(1) Download the free Linguacious® scanner* on your smartphone or tablet device and use it to scan each QR code: www.linguacious.net/scanner

(2) Visit the Audio section on our website or scan this code:

*Our scanner app is the only one that works well with our QR codes. Requires an active Internet connection.

Page Design

The language elements on each page are:

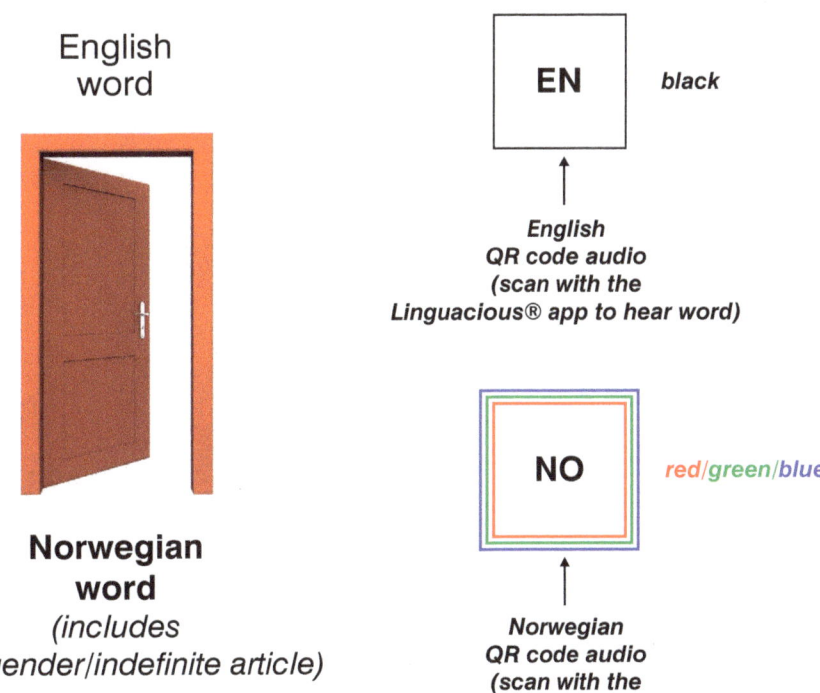

backpack

en ryggsekk

ball

SCAN ME

SCAN ME

en ball

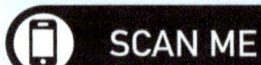

bed

en seng

book

en bok

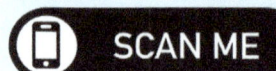

box

en boks

chair

en stol

clock

en klokke

couch

en sofa

cup

en kopp

door

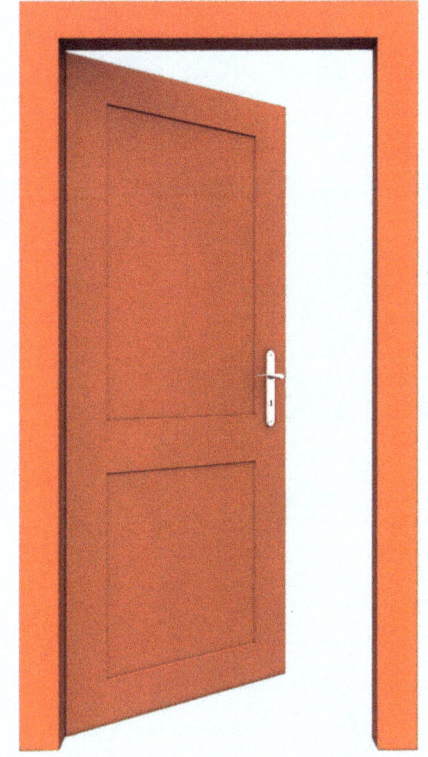

en dør

dress

en kjole

fan

SCAN ME

SCAN ME

en vifte

fork

en gaffel

fridge

et kjøleskap

gift

en gave

glass

et glass

glasses

briller

 key

en nøkkel

knife

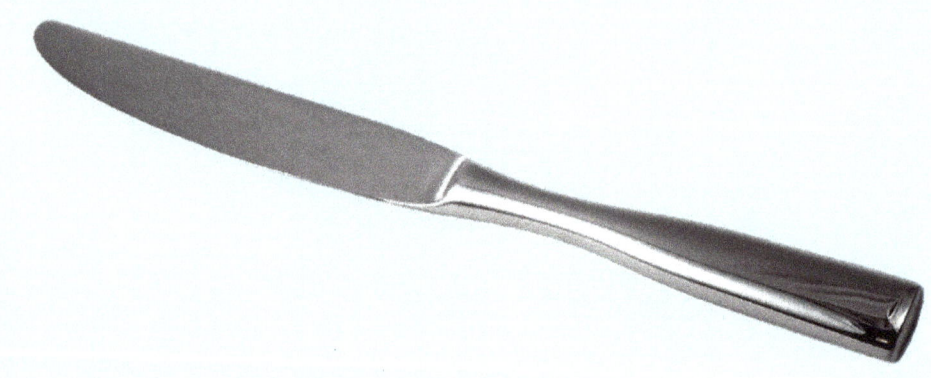

en kniv

microwave

en mikrobølgeovn

pants

en bukse

pen

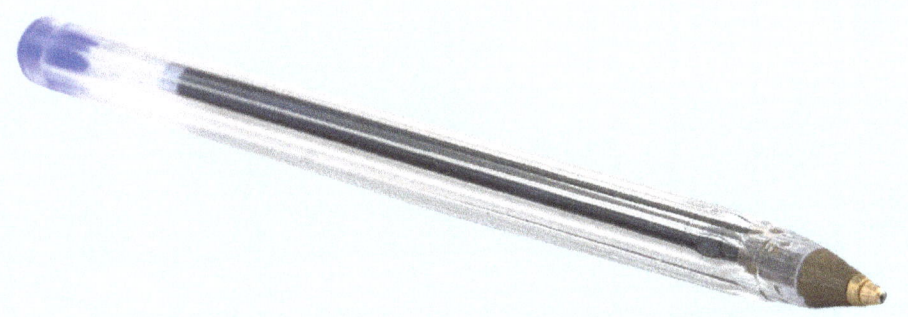

en penn

plate

en tallerken

scissors

en saks

shirt

en skjorte

shoes

SCAN ME

SCAN ME

sko

socks

sokker

spoon

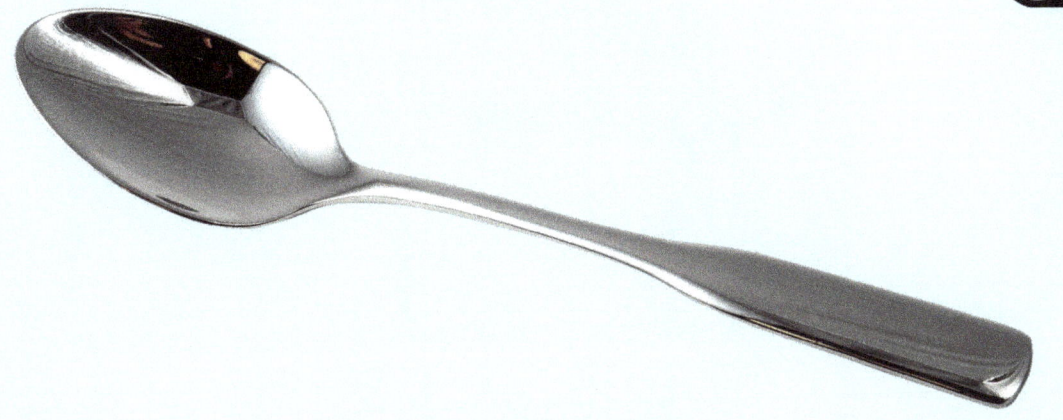

en skje

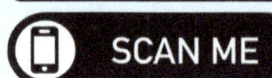

table

et bord

# television

en TV

toilet

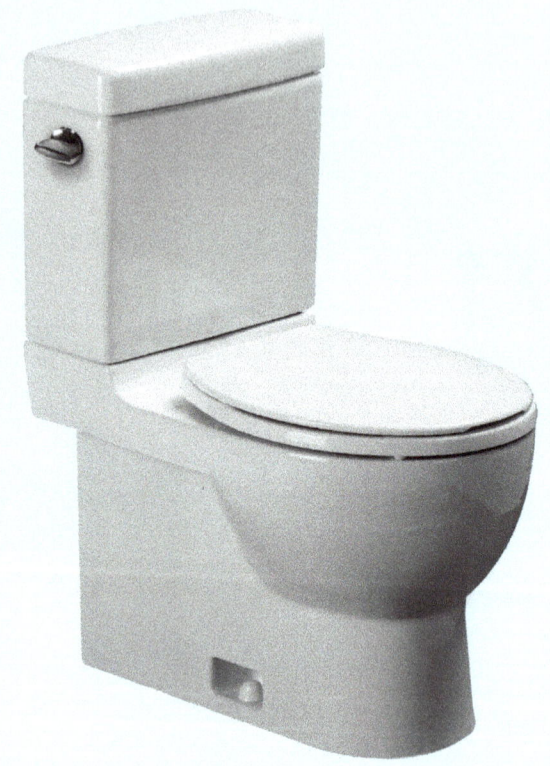

et toalett

toothbrush

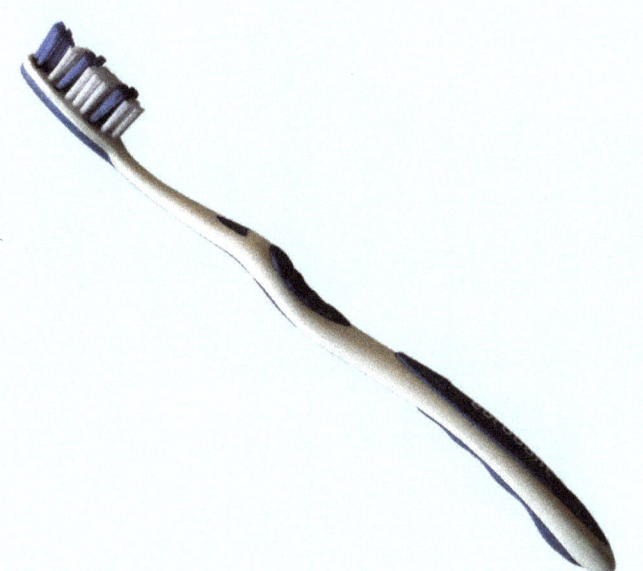

en tannbørste

towel

et håndkle

toys

leker

trash can

en søppelbøtte

t-shirt

en T-skjorte

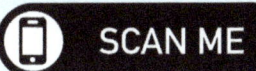

vacuum cleaner

en støvsuger

 washing machine

en vaskemaskin

WORD GAMES

Would you like to practice the words in this book with some free printable games?

Simply visit the link below and have fun!

www.linguacious.net/littlepolyglot-games

If you liked this book, please kindly leave a product review. Your review will help this book stay available and will help others discover and benefit from it as well. Thank you so much!

CPSIA information can be obtained
at www.ICGtesting.com
Printed in the USA
BVHW091224090321
602113BV00019B/1995